Presented

to

_____

_____

by

_____

_____

_____
DATE

TO

My own partner in the great adventure

All those who assist young people in the process of building successful marriages

All my students — past, present, and future — in the course in courtship and marriage

U.W.M. who said that one day I would write a book of this type.

Louis O. Caldwell

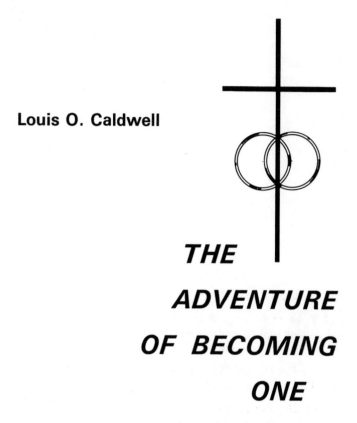

THE
ADVENTURE
OF BECOMING
ONE

Baker Book House ● Grand Rapids, Michigan

ACKNOWLEDGMENTS

Judi Treat and Peggy Branscum, able and patient typists, without whose help my work would go unfinished.

LaVerne L. Carmical, Professor of Counselor Education, University of Houston

Gordon De Young, who provides the kind of editorial help that makes working with him a genuine pleasure.

ISBN: 0-8010-2334-3
Library of Congress Card Catalog Number: 69-16930
Copyright 1969 by Baker Book House Company
Eighth printing, October 1981
Printed in the United States of America

Contents

And the Lord God said, it is not good that the man should be alone; I will make an help meet for him.

— Genesis 2:18

. . . He which made them at the beginning made them male and female, and said, For this cause shall a man leave father and mother, and shall cleave to his wife: and they twain shall be one flesh.

— Matthew 19:4, 5

The Adventure Begins 1

"With this ring I thee wed . . . ." Speaking these words, you realize you are standing on the tallest peak of the mountain range of human relationships.

You and your companion at the altar have climbed to the heights of mutual commitment. Now with every fiber of your being, you have entered into the spirit of what Elizabeth Barrett Browning expressed in these memorable lines:

> How do I love thee? Let me count the ways.
> I love thee to the depth and breadth and height
> My soul can reach, when feeling out of sight
> For the ends of Being and ideal Grace.
> I love thee to the level of every day's
> Most quiet need, by sun and candlelight.
> I love thee purely, as they turn from Praise.
> I love thee freely, as men strive for Right;
> I love thee with the passion put to use
> In my old griefs, and with my childhood's faith.

> I love thee with a love I seemed to lose
> With my lost saints — I love thee with the breath,
> Smiles, tears, of all my life! — and, if God choose,
> I shall but love thee better after death.[1]

Your courtship period was an experience in learning to relate to your partner in various ways and situations. Each of you was discovering more about himself and the other. Gradually you came to assess your life values and goals and those of your future mate. Together you developed until each of you decided, "I have found the one with whom I wish to live the rest of my life." If your courtship was typical, this realization came in spite of the sometimes rocky and painful nature of the climb. Just as your courtship period was an uncertain journey, so your marriage can be a creative adventure. When used in describing what the nature of "becoming one" can be, the word *adventure* means much more than the dictionary's definition — "an exciting or unusual experience" (Webster).

Let's take adventure to mean direction rather than destination, possibilities instead of limitations, opportunity to achieve and contribute, not confinement by narrow controls and restrictions.

Of course, you are not unaware that this concept is ridiculed by others who have written about it facetiously or cynically.

> Needles and pins, needles and pins,
> When a man marries his troubles begin.
> — Anonymous

> If you want a good year marry;
> If you want two, refrain.
> — German Proverb

> I would advise a man to pause
> Before he takes a wife;
> In fact I see no earthly cause
> He shouldn't pause for life.
> — de Marivaux

> Marriage is reaching into a bag of snakes
> In the hope of catching an eel.
> — Spanish Proverb

> Bigamy is having one mate too many.
> Monogamy is the same.
> — Anonymous

We know there are those who see marriage as a book in which the first chapter emphasizes the first syllable in wedlock, the remaining chapters the second syllable. Added to this is the statistic that a fraction over one out of every four marriages in America ends in divorce. Incredibly enough, the institution of marriage is being re-evaluated by a few radical thinkers who are questioning its usefulness and desirability.

We have only to turn to the Book of Books to get the truth about marriage:

> The Lord God said, it is not good that the man should live alone; I will make him a help meet for him.
> — Genesis 2:18

> Whoso findeth a wife findeth a good thing, and obtaineth favor of the Lord. — Proverbs 18:22

> Marriage is honorable in all. — Hebrews 13:4

"Marriages are made in heaven," someone once said. One wiser than he had this insight: "Marriages are recognized in heaven but must be worked out on earth." The Christian marriage ceremony is designed to create a heightened awareness of heaven's role. The symbolism, songs, vows and prayers are sacred and solemn reminders of the spiritual nature of the union formed at the altar. That your marriage has "heavenly recognition" is evidenced by Christ's statement that husband and wife are joined together by God (Mark 10:9).

Remember, too, that Christ's first miracle was performed at a wedding in Cana of Galilee. By His holy presence He hallowed the marriage union. By His holy power He supplied the guests with additional wine. He thus spared the bridegroom great embarrassment and became the life of the party! His blessing upon your marriage can change the water of ordinary married life to the wine of adventure!

Divine blessing of your marriage, however, does not lessen the need for human cooperation if your union is to become an adventure. It has been humorously observed that marriage is like a violin. After the music stops, the strings are still attached. Is it possible for any relationship "with strings attached" to be an adventure? According to Dr. Paul Tournier, adventure is not to be understood in terms of emotional peaks and absence of struggle. He sees the law of adventure operating in the continual dying of even our most exciting adventure. In fact adventure must die, he believes, in order to be born again! In the death and rebirth of adventure we grow and mature and are prepared for other adventures resulting in greater meaning and fruitfulness. Dr. Tournier writes, "Marriage is

. . . an excellent instrument for the constant renewal of adventure, at once both stimulating to the personal development of each of the partners and enriching to the union."[2]

To illustrate this point, Dr. Tournier relates a personal experience regarding the publication of his first book. He met with a group of friends to get their impressions of his manuscript. They not only advised him against attempting to publish it, but also expressed grave doubts about the wisdom of his plans to slant his life's work toward exploring the role that spiritual and moral life play in health, disease and healing. Understandably shaken by the group's reaction, the Swiss psychiatrist returned home. His wife so effectively bolstered his sagging spirits that he decided to take the daring risk. The effect of this encouragement on his relationship with his wife is described in the good doctor's own words: "From then on it had been not *my* adventure but *ours.*" He added, "Happy is the marriage in which both husband and wife live the same adventure together. It is astonishing how it strengthens the bonds uniting them."[3]

We know only too well that marriage as an adventure is not always a reality, but it *is* possible. Your wedding is the commencement of this possibility, not its guarantee. And isn't it true that possibilities ignite the spirit of adventure, especially if your choice of a life's companion offers the promise contained in the lines:

> Believe me, if all those endearing young charms,
>> Which I gaze on so fondly today,
> Were to change by tomorrow, and fleet in my arms,
>> Like fairy-gifts fading away,

Thou wouldst still be adored, as this moment thou art,
   Let thy loveliness fade as it will,
And around the dear ruin each wish of my heart
   Would entwine itself verdantly still.

It is not while beauty and youth are thine own,
   And my cheeks unprofaned by a tear,
That the fervor and faith of a soul may be known,
   To which time will make thee more dear!
No, the heart that has truly lov'd never forgets,
   But as truly loves on to the close;
As the sunflower turns to her god, when he sets,
   The same look which she turn'd when he rose!

— Thomas Moore

This is the kind of love that "many waters cannot quench, neither can the floods drown it . . . (Song of Solomon 8:7).

Notes

1. From *Sonnets From The Portuguese*
2. Paul Tournier, *The Adventure of Living*: Harper and Row, p. 68
3. Ibid., p. 49

The Significance of Becoming 2

Perhaps the best way to begin this chapter would be to say, "Don't read it until you feel your getting married must have been a mistake." For unlike the Pilgrim's journey to the promised land, the adventure of becoming one starts with the Delectable Mountain and then faces the Slough of Despond, Doubting Castle and Giant Despair.

As a young man, Theodore Roosevelt said, "What I am going to be, I am now becoming." That is not only true of individuals but of marriage relationships as well. If left to chance, luck, or fate, will you and your mate "live happily ever after"?

Newlyweds often become disillusioned with married life. "Right after I married," confessed one man, "I wondered if I'd made a mistake. Now after some

Two Lovers

Two lovers by a moss-grown spring:
They leaned soft cheeks together there,
Mingled the dark and sunny hair,
and heard the wooing thrushes sing.
    Oh budding time!
    O love's blest prime!

Two wedded from the portal stept;
The bells made happy carolings,
The air was soft as fanning wings,
White petals on the pathway slept.
    O pure-eyed bride!
    O tender pride!

Two faces o'er a cradle bent;
Two hands above the head were locked;
These pressed each other while they rocked;
Those watched a life that love had sent.
    O solemn hour!
    O hidden power!

Two parents by the evening fire;
The red light fell about their knees
On heads that rose by slow degrees
Like buds upon the lily spire.

O patient life!
O tender strife!

The two still sat together there,
The red light fell about their knees
But all the heads by slow degrees
Had gone and left the lonely pair.

O voyage fast!
O vanished past!

The red light shone upon the floor
And made the space between them wide;
They drew their chairs up side by side,
Their pale cheeks joined and said,

"Once more!"
O memories!
O past that is!

— George Eliot

twenty years, I realize that I've married the best wife in the world." Usually the reason for such premature evaluations is that of unrealistic expectations. One prominent marriage counselor contends that marital difficulty is primarily the result of expecting too much of early marriage and expecting too little late in marriage.[1]

One young bride of less than a year sadly shook her head as she related to me how miserable she was. "I just don't understand how something so wonderful could turn out to be such a disappointment," she said. "Was there any love left?" she wondered. "Can my marriage still be successful?"

I answered by telling her a story of a powerful monarch in ancient times who called his counselors to his side one day. "Listen carefully," he began, "for I have a most important task for you. I need a saying to place on my royal ring. This saying must be appropriate for any problem that might be brought to me." After some days had passed, the counselors returned with their solution. When the monarch heard it, he was well pleased with his counselors' wisdom. The saying? "For this, too, shall pass."

The distraught young wife pondered the saying and then looked at me with new hope in her eyes. She had understood.

Recall the title of this book. It would have been a serious mistake to title it, *The Adventure of Being One.* For oneness is not attained at the wedding; it is a process that continues throughout life. An understanding of this concept is vital, especially when the marriage relationship seems more like a tragedy than an

just to know that the trouble can be "tem-
... s one the courage to keep trying. Young
... n weather the storms that occasionally come
... ng themselves that "This, too, shall pass."
The kind of love that makes possible a marriage such
as George Eliot described in her poem, "Two Lovers"
is a love that continues to grow.

Another helpful point to remember is that your marriage is moving in some direction. In answering the
question, what is it that husbands and wives want, or
should want, a famous psychiatrist suggests four things:
First, a partner who shares our life, including our sorrows and joys, our failures and our successes; next,
the development of a home and becoming a parent;
third, a rich and rewarding personal life that derives
satisfaction, security and achievement; fourth, a sense
of direction — is it for "better" or for "worse"? Which
direction do you want it to go? What are your goals?[2]
How truly spoke he who said, "No wind is favorable
if the captain does not know toward which port he is
steering." If indeed it is true that your marriage is always in the process of becoming, what is it becoming?

There are many noble goals that might be set up:
Deepening love for one another, responsible parenthood, expanding social relationships, economic stability, and many others. Someone has said that marriage
offers a unique opportunity for the couple to become
friends. Perhaps love could be defined as friendship
grown up, tested and triumphant.

> I love you, not only for what you are, but for what
> I am when I am with you.
> I love you, not only for what you have made of your-

self, but for what you are making of me.

I love you for the part of me that you bring out.

I love you for putting your hand into my heaped-up
heart and passing over all the frivolous and weak
things that you cannot help seeing there and drawing out into the light all the beautiful, radiant things
that no one else has looked quite far enough to
find.

I love you for ignoring the possibilities of the fool in
me and laying firm hold of the possibilities of good
in me.

I love you for closing your eyes to the discords in me
and for adding to the music in me by worshipful
listening.

I love you because you are helping me to make of the
lumber of my life, not a tavern, but a temple, and of
the words of my days, not a reproach, but a song.

I love you because you have done more than any creed
could have done to make me happy.

You have done it without a touch, without a word, without a sign.

You have done it by being yourself.

After all, perhaps this is what being a friend means.

— Mary Carolyn Davies

Essentially, the Christian couple are concerned with
seeking to know and do the will of God in their lives
within the context of the maturing marriage. Admit-
tedly, the intelligent questions relative to the "process
of becoming" are: What do I want to become person-
ally, and what do I want my marriage to become?
These questions should be answered in terms of what
you sincerely believe to be God's will for you and your
marriage.

Does this represent a conflict between human and
Divine wills? To illustrate the solution to this prob-

lem, a certain father told of one of his sons, about eight or ten years old, who liked to have his own way. "Phillip, you ought not to want your own way," he said to the boy one day. Phillip thought about his father's statement and then asked, "Father, if I choose the will of the Lord and go His way because I want to, don't I still have my way?" Augustine said, "Love God and do what you will." This is the secret of successful Christian living that more perceptive saints have long realized. When hearts are united in common commitment to Christ, the Divine and human wills are harmonized.

Third, when you consider how each partner has developed uniquely you begin to understand why the early months of marriage can be quite trying. The way you react to conflict, stress, frustration; that dominant way of behaving that makes you identifiable — call it life style or life pattern — is different from that of your mate. Coming together is bound to create adjustment problems.

Those who have sought to illustrate this concept often point to that which happens when two streams of water converge. There is a certain amount of turbulence created at the point of convergence. As the flow of water is carried along, however, you can observe evidence that the two separate streams have merged. Now there is new power in the flow, less turbulence and greater potential for creative use.

An experience of Ike and Mamie Eisenhower illustrates this well. When the Eisenhowers celebrated their 50th wedding anniversary (1966) they were asked about marital bickering. General Eisenhower flashed his famous smile and said that he thought it is an ever-present part of marriage, adding, "But there's this about it. The older you grow the less important they are. At first I suppose the first difficulty you ever had you thought your wife didn't love you any more and you wanted to take off to Argentina. But now . . . I think differences of opinion . . . disappear very quickly."

Perhaps Ike was remembering some experiences in his early married life that were like one I recently heard about. A student told me of working with a certain young man who stated one day that he and his wife had had a quarrel before he left for work one morning. At noon, when they sat down to eat lunch, he unwrapped a sandwich and bit into it. A strange look came on his face. Inside the sandwich was a note saying, "I'm still mad at you!"[3]

A young man was leaving for college and was talking to his pastor. "Just promise me you'll have the good sense of a cow," counseled the pastor.

"I'm not sure I follow you," replied the youth.

"Well," explained the pastor, "when you throw a cow some hay, she has the good sense to know that she must separate the hay from the sticks. She eats the hay and leaves the sticks."

The hay-and-sticks principle can be profitably applied to the young marriage relationship that is in the process of becoming. Until they are properly evaluated, many marital arguments are over mere "sticks." A sense of what is important develops with time as we grow in ability to recognize the differences between "hay" and "sticks" in the affairs of life.

One final point: The establishing of goals is necessary, but there is a danger involved. Carlyle's dictum reveals it to us. He said, "Our major business is not to see what lies dimly at a distance, but to do what clearly lies at hand."

The pattern of the future of your marriage is not developed by dreams and goals but by your present behavior. Only by *being* what we ought to be *NOW* can we hope to *become* what we dream of becoming later.

Therefore, we do well to heed the advice of the sage who wrote:

> Listen to the Exhortation of the Dawn!
>   Look to this Day!
> For it is Life, the very Life of Life.
> In its brief course lie all the Verities and Realities of
>   your Existence:
>   The Bliss of Growth,
>   The Glory of Action,
>   The Splendor of Beauty.
> For Yesterday is but a Dream,
> And To-morrow is only a Vision;
> But To-day well-lived makes every Yesterday a Dream
>   of Happiness,
> And every To-morrow a Vision of Hope.
> Look well therefore to this Day!
> Such is the Salutation of the Dawn.
>   — *The Salutation of the Dawn,* from the *Sanskrit*

Notes

1. David R. Mace, *Success In Marriage*: Abingdon
2. William C. Menninger, *Living In A Troubled World*
3. Contributed by Marvin Swift

3 | It Takes Three to Make One

One of the most tender passages in the opening book of the Bible reveals the Divine recognition of man's profound loneliness apart from his mate: "And the Lord God said, it is not good that the man should be alone; I will make a help meet for him" (Genesis 2: 18). The creative work that followed is described further in the same chapter:

And the Lord God caused a deep sleep to fall upon Adam, and he slept: and he took one of his ribs, and closed up the flesh instead thereof;

And the rib, which the Lord God had taken from man, made he a woman, and brought her unto the man.

And Adam said, This is now bone of my bones, and flesh of my flesh: she shall be called woman, because she was taken out of man.

Therefore shall a man leave his father and his mother, and shall cleave unto his wife: and they shall be one flesh.

— Genesis 2:21-24

Recently, a colleague was talking to me about his marriage. He had left his wife for a three-week period to teach in a summer school several hundred miles from their home. "After five years of marriage," he reflected, "I've just begun to realize the meaning of the idea of oneness. I've been away from my wife just a few days and I feel as if a part of me is missing."

This concept of oneness in marriage is unique to the marriage relationship. It offers opportunity for fulfillment and completeness. It involves both the giving of oneself and the receiving of the mate. Some see marriage as the process of becoming one all right, but the only trouble is that neither can determine which one! Perhaps "sharing" carries a major part of the secret.

> We have had our little sorrows,
>> We have known our little pain;
> We have had our dark tomorrows,
>> Had our sunshine after rain.
>
> But the worst of all our losses,
>> Loyal comrade of my heart,
> We have found the little crosses
>> That we tried to bear apart!
>
> Care we jointly bore proved blessing;
>> Care each bore alone proved blight —
> Till, with humble, frank confessing,
>> Each returned to each for light;
>
> Till we learned the law unfailing
>> That controls our happiness:

IT TAKES THREE TO MAKE ONE   23

Prayers and tears of unavailing
　　Prayed or shed in selfishness.

Then, though bleak or blithe the weather,
　　Be the landscape gray or green,
Let us cling so close together,
　　Not a care can creep between.
　　　　　　　　— Strickland W. Gillilan

Becoming one, in the finest sense, involves sharing more than joys and sorrows. According to the sociologist J. D. Unwin, a marriage can never fully mature unless the partners share an allegiance to some purpose outside themselves which they considered to be ultimately more important than themselves or their relationships.

Actually, mature love is a great alchemy created by goals and purposes that are mutually attractive. This concept is not as generally understood as it needs to be. As Antoine De Saint-Exupeiry said, "True love does not consist in gazing at each other, but looking outward together in the same direction."

This focuses attention on the crux of the matter. Becoming increasingly one on the human level is a potential relationship that can be actualized only as each partner grows in conformity to the image of Christ. The problem must go beyond finding *something* to live for, to finding *someone* to live for. The great principle underlying the deepest kind of merging of husband and wife has not to do with mere physical relations, things, circumstances, philosophy or vague mysticism. Only mutual commitment to Christ enables human beings to transcend their weaknesses and grow increasingly in oneness. The exalting result is that as they get closer and closer to Christ they get closer and closer to each other. The great principle then is this: It takes *three* to make one — you, your mate and the living Christ.

One of the most beautiful tributes to a wife came from the pen of Charles H. Spurgeon, whose wife realized, along with her husband, the opportunity for the excelling oneness that Christ offers. Spurgeon wrote:

> She delights in her husband, in his person, his character, his affection; to her, he is not only the chief and foremost of mankind, but in her eyes, he is all in all. Her heart's love belongs to him and to him only. . . . She is glad to sink her individuality in his. She seeks no renown for herself; his honor is reflected upon her, she rejoices in it. She will defend his name with her dying breath; safe enough is he where she can speak for him. His smiling gratitude is all the reward she seeks. Even in her dress she thinks of him, and considers nothing beautiful which is distasteful to him. He has many objects in life, some of which she does not quite understand; but she believes in them all, and anything she can do to promote them, she delights to perform . . . Such a wife, as a true spouse, realizes the model marriage relation, and sets forth what our oneness with the Lord ought to be!

By now we have come to see that the Christian marriage is best understood in terms of a radically new orientation to life. "If any man be in Christ," said Paul, "he is a new creature: old things are passed away; behold, all things are become new" (II Corinthians 5:17). The non-Christian marriage depends upon love for each other; the Christian marriage upon love for Christ. The non-Christian marriage is concerned with satisfactions that are temporary, limited to this life; the Christian marriage with things that are eternal, embracing this life and the life to come. The non-Christian marriage has the resources of human nature; the Christian marriage, the resources of Christ's Divine nature through the ministry of the Holy Spirit.

Certain corollaries are derived from the principle that says it takes three to become one.

1. The marriage relationship is a lasting one. Dr. Alfred Kinsey cited a preliminary examination of 6,000 marital histories and of nearly 3,000 divorce histories. In his opinion this study suggests that there may be nothing more important in a marriage than a determination that it shall persist. Ann Bys cleverly put it like this: "Fewer marriages would skid, if those who said 'I do' — did." These are respectable solutions but there is a greater basis for marriage stability. If *both* partners desire to please Christ above everything else, then God's will for the union will be achieved. As each mate conforms more and more to the image of Christ, the union between them becomes stronger and more satisfying. Inherent in this kind of union are those qualities that provide for enduring stability. It can only be said of Christians that when they marry, they start something they cannot stop.

2. The relationship that absorbs both partners in such a way that they become "one," is dynamic, that is, it requires both partners to continue to grow as individual Christians. This means that by its very nature a

successful marriage is never a point to be reached but a process to be nourished.

A deeply moving episode is found in Bunyan's classic *The Pilgrim's Progress*. When Pilgrim was asked by Charity, "Why did you not bring your wife along with you?" he sobbingly replied, "Oh how willingly would I have done it, but she was averse to my going on a pilgrimage."

How different was the attitude of the lovely young lady who became the wife of the great D. L. Moody. As the twenty-three-year-old Moody's ministry was ripening, he and Emma Charlotte Revell, just seventeen, found their relationship ripening too. At Moody's tender proposal, Charlotte answered in the unforgettable words of Ruth:

> Where thou goest, I will go,
> Where thou lodgest, I will lodge.

So well did she live up to this avowal that when she passed from this life, it was said of her: "She found the greatest joy in the circle of her home and family, yet when duty called her to the responsibilities of social life, her natural grace and culture were admired by everybody. . . . She made her home the best place on earth for her family. . . . Everyone understood her wise counsel and support was one of the secrets of D. L. Moody's success."

Does being absorbed in the marriage union result in the loss of self? Those who protest that they will lose their individuality have missed the secret to finding themselves. The surest way to fail to find oneself is to set up self-discovery as a goal. The discovery and development of individuality is achieved interpersonally, never apart from others. Again, the spiritual dimension holds the answer: "He that findeth his life shall lose it: and he that loseth his life for my sake shall find it" (Matthew 10:39).

3. Achieving the highest degree of oneness, fusion, union, harmony, is impossible unless a truly Christian kind of human relationship is set up as a goal, for human nature is weak and the heart deceitful. Lofty ideals are vital and dreams of "what can be" are ennobling. However, the sad story of human history is that unconverted man, even with all his ideals and dreams, lacks the one force necessary to fulfillment — the ability to transcend his weakness.

In his splendid little volume simply entitled *Marriage*, the late Dr. William Lyon Phelps wrote:

> I suggest to those recently married and those about to be married that they are entering into a relationship that can bring them the highest and most lasting happiness or the most crushing disillusion and despair. Such a relationship is particularly remarkable because of its intimacy, and intimacy far transcending that of friendship, love of parents or any earthly emotion. As Thomas Hardy said, "Marriage annihilates reserve." In this amazing intimacy, every care should be taken to ensure success. A common interest in religion, saying prayers together, will help enormously toward increasing and preserving happiness.

Human weakness and immaturity find quick exposure in the demanding relationship of marriage. The kind of patience, unselfishness, openness and understanding needed for a great marriage demand resources that are spiritual. Christians are made aware of the unlimited resources available in the living Christ by the ministry of the Holy Spirit. Marriage finds renewal, empowerment, and becomes an adventure when Christ is real to both partners. Because the most serious problems are spiritual, it follows that the indwelling of the Holy Spirit is more essential than mere knowledge. We are only too painfully aware that our behavior is not controlled and directed solely in terms of what we know. Successful adjustment to married life depends more upon *whom* we know rather than *what* we know. This is not to minimize the importance of education and continued search for knowledge. It is an attempt to *recognize* the facts about human nature.

The Persians have a story about a powerful Eastern monarch named Fafer who reigned in the Kingdom of Serendip (Ceylon). Fafer had three sons whom he carefully schooled with an eye toward the day when they would succeed him in his dominions. To broaden their education, he sent them out to travel in other lands. As they journeyed, the three young princes discovered many valuable things for which they were not seeking.

In 1754, Sir Horace Walpole was pondering the meaning of the legend of the *Three Princes of Serendip*. He thought about the frequency with which many people have made surprising discoveries when they were seeking something else. And so Sir Horace coined the term *serendipity*, meaning "the gift of finding valuable or agreeable things not sought for."

J. Wallace Hamilton insightfully points out in his book entitled *Serendipity*[1] that the greatest of all serendipities was given by Christ. When He said, "Seek ye first the kingdom of God, and his righteousness," Christ added that the valuable and necessary things in life would be by-products — "and all *these things* shall be added unto you" (Matthew 6:33).

In a general sense, marital success is a great serendipity. It is a by-product of seeking to do the will of God in daily behavior, living, planning, spending, evaluating, choosing. The serendipity concept of marriage provides another way of understanding that "the adventure of becoming one" depends upon something other than human ability. Only as the marriage becomes increasingly Christ-centered can marriage partners experience the "serendipity" of achieving growing oneness.

Married partners who understand this get more from the altar than the unconverted receive from being on the psychiatrist's couch. Marriage puts weights on some, wings on others. Being truly baptized in the Holy Spirit makes the great difference. A close reading of the Book of Acts would show us why. Dr. William Culbertson, President of Moody Bible Institute, has pointed out what happens when one is possessed by the Holy Spirit. He states:

> He who is the Spirit of truth, of grace, of holiness, of life, and of glory will produce these qualities in the life of the man or the woman who is filled with the Spirit. To be filled with the Spirit and to be a liar is not possible; He is the Spirit of truth. To be filled with the Spirit and to be bitter, hateful, and ungracious is not possible; He is

the Spirit of grace. To be filled with the Spirit and to be sensual, unclean, worldly, is not possible; He is the Spirit of holiness. To be filled with the Spirit and to be spiritually cold and even lukewarm is not possible; He is the Spirit of life.

The implications of these truths for married couples is obvious.

The kind of oneness of which this chapter speaks is the ideal. As such, it can never be completely achieved. Thus every day and every noble effort can contribute to getting nearer the ideal. And this is what nourishes the adventure.

Notes

1. J. Wallace Hamilton, *Serendipity*: Fleming H. Revell, 1965

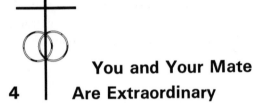

4 You and Your Mate Are Extraordinary

I have heard of a bride who appeared at the altar with her hair in curlers. When asked why she replied, "Because I want to look good for the reception!"

This kind of distorted thinking is not confined to brides, either! A young husband was telling me about his marital problems. He repeated over and over, "I don't understand why my wife doesn't see things differently." What he meant was, of course, she didn't agree with him and he couldn't entertain the possibility that he could be wrong. Didn't the poet include all of us when he penned:

> In matters controversial
> My perception's always fine —
> I always see both points of view —
> The one that's wrong and mine!

Basic to handling problems between persons is this fundamental fact: We see things not as they are, but as we are. And how are we? Until husband and wife clearly understand this point, the future of the marriage relationship cannot be promising.

A good place to start is with this insight of professor Mark Van Doren's: "These are two statements about human beings that are true: That all human beings are alike, and that all are different." Thus the famous professor underscores the significance of bisexuality.

To dismiss the fact that the human race is comprised of two types of beings — male and female — is a mistake that strikes at the foundation of marital success.

"God created man in his own image . . . male and female created he them" (Genesis 1:27). Another writer of a generation far removed reflected on the human creation and was moved to write, "I am fearfully and wonderfully made" (Psalms 139:14).

From these truths Christian newlyweds derive their deepest sense of acceptance of and honor for themselves and their mates.

How are the sexes alike? Perhaps the answer can be most clearly stated in terms of needs. Aside from the self-evident physiological needs — food, air, water, warmth — it may be said that both men and women need love, sexual fulfillment, security, acceptance, appreciation, success, meaning for life, forgiveness, hope, eternal life. A prominent psychiatrist has reduced psychological needs to two. First is the need to love and to be loved; second is the need to feel that you are a person of worth, and that other people feel this way about you.

Now consider some differences — not with respect to being male or female, but with respect to being human. A book[1] written by Roger J. Williams, professor of biochemistry at the University of Texas, reveals some startling facts about human individuality. Dr. Williams indicates that wide variations exist in stomachs, hearts, glands, sense of timing, nervous systems, brains, personalities, temperaments, sleep patterns. You and your mate are truly as unique as fingerprints, built in highly distinctive ways in every particular.

When both husband and wife understand these differences, their relationships are greatly improved. Dr. Williams explains that "little things" are often responsible for tearing people apart. He mentions individual reactions to temperature: "coffee or soups may be too hot or not hot enough; rooms may be too hot or too cold or too stuffy; bed covering may be too warm or too light."

What differences exist relative to maleness and femaleness? The husband claims to be the wife's physical superior, but she may counter with a reminder that women have greater resistance to disease and death and to emotional pressure. In America seven out of every ten husbands die before their wives.

> The weaker sex is understood
> To mean the whole of womanhood;
> But I have yet to find a man
> Who knows whom it is weaker than.
> — Anonymous

Another poet has observed:

> A woman may be small of frame
> With tiny feet that patter,
> But when she puts one small foot down
> Her shoe size doesn't matter.
>
> — Anonymous

This position might be challenged by members of the fairer sex. Are the ladies gaining control? One thinks not and says so in this bit of delightful verse:

> Oh, it's a man's world, and for man it's rosy.
> For men *investigate;* women are *nosy.*
> Men *stand firm;* but women are *mulish.*
> The male's *indiscreet;* the female's *foolish.*
> A man takes *credit;* a woman is *bragging.*
> A man is *critical;* a woman is *nagging.*
> Men make *concessions;* women *surrender.*
> But nevertheless, the feminine gender
> Has one advantage it well deserves:
> Men have *tempers;* but women have *nerves.*

As individuals mature, sex differences in aptitudes begin to become more pronounced. Results of psychological tests indicate that men do better in mechanical skills, mathematical reasoning and comprehension of abstract meanings. On the other hand women do better in language skills, hand skills, social knowledge, perception and memory. That the sexes think differently is emphasized by results of intelligence tests. Men seem to value the theoretical, economic, political, abstract and powerful, whereas, women's values lie in the areas of the aesthetic, social and religious. Generally, men are aggressive, dominant and active; women are more passive, docile, socially dependent, self-centered. Men are oriented toward achievement, ideas, administration, while women are oriented toward finding fulfillment through people.

Obviously, sex differences are a product of interaction between heredity and culture. Therefore, the wise question is not who is superior or inferior, but how can these differences be utilized to contribute to the development of the marriage relationship? One whose understanding of human nature is widely respected has written:

> The fallacy of the inferiority of woman and its corollary, the superiority of man, constantly disturb the harmony of the sexes."[2]

He notes that the tension produced by this disharmony poisons, distorts and corrodes the total love life of husband and wife.

A pioneer in the field of marriage counseling was speaking in India to a Hindu group. When he asked the group what happens in a typical Hindu home when husband and wife disagree, this baffling reply was given: "That never happens."

"Why not," came the challenge.

The explanation traced the kind of training given the little Hindu girl. She is brought up to believe that her husband will be to her a god. Therefore, when she grows up and marries, her husband can do or say nothing wrong. So there is no reason to disagree.

A scanning of human history reveals that the plight of the married woman has been such that she has been forced to make most of the adjustments in marriage. The extent to which her legal rights were recognized even as late as the 1800's is pointed out in a classic statement by Sir William Blackstone:

By marriage, the husband and the wife are one person in law; that is, the very being or legal existence of the woman is suspended during the marriage, or at least is incorporated and consolidated into that of her husband. . . . Upon this principle of a union of person in husband and wife depend almost all the legal rights, duties and disabilities that either of them acquire by the marriage. . . . For this reason a man cannot grant anything to his wife, or enter in to covenant with her; for the grant would be to suppose her separate existence and to covenant with her would only be to covenant with himself; and therefore it is also generally true that all arrangements made between husband and wife when single are voided by the inter-marriage.[3]

Scripture, not society, should be our standard for identifying the roles and functions of husbands and wives. Obedience to Christ instead of conformity to culture is the only way we can clear the confusion in this vital area. Ponder these Biblical admonitions:

For Husbands:

Husbands, love your wives, even as Christ also loved the church, and gave himself for it. — Ephesians 5:25

Husbands love your wives, and be not bitter against them. — Colossians 3:19

Likewise, ye husbands, dwell with them according to knowledge, giving honor unto the wife, as unto the weaker vessel, and as being heirs together of the grace

For Wives:

Wives, submit yourselves unto your own husbands, as unto the Lord. For the husband is the head of the Wife, even as Christ is the head of the Church; and he is the savior of the body. Therefore as the church is subject unto Christ, so let the wives be subject to their own husbands in everything. — Ephesians 5:22-24

Likewise, ye wives, be in subjection to your own hus-

of life; that your prayers be not hindered — I Peter 3:7

bands; that, if any obey not the word, they also may without the word be won by the conversation of the wives; While they behold your chaste conversation coupled with fear — I Peter 3:1-2

A distressed young husband approached the late Dr. Ironside, pastor of the famed Moody Church in Chicago, and confessed that he was "drifting into idolatry." When asked to explain his problem, the young man told of how deeply he loved his beautiful young bride. His concern was that he was putting her on too high a plane and loving her too much. Was he displeasing the Lord in so doing?

Dr. Ironside answered, "Do you love your wife more than Christ loved the Church?"

"I don't think so," responded the young man.

"Well," said the wise pastor, "that is the limit, for we read, 'Husbands love your wives, even as Christ also loved the church, and gave himself for it.'"[4]

Billy Graham makes a practice of including sermons on family life in his crusade messages. In these sermons he refers to the Biblical statement about husbands being head of the house. Does he practice this?

One of Graham's biographers cites a rather rocky romantic period just before Billy and Ruth's wedding. Ruth's ambition was to be a pioneer missionary to Tibet. She knew that Billy had no such leading from God. Discussing these uncertainties led Billy to inquire of her, "Well, do you think God brought us together?" She admitted she did. Then pointed out

Billy, "The Bible clearly teaches that the husband is the head of the wife. The Lord leads me and you follow," he explained. Ruth consented, "in faith."

A clear understanding of the Divine order of responsibility and privilege of both husband and wife leads to cooperation not competition. Mature adults are sensitive to needs, moods and circumstances within the context of family life. Their behavior is guided by a higher order of principles rather than by stereotyped ideas of what a "man ought to do" or what a "woman ought to do."

The complementary nature of the two sexes has been obscured by individual behavior and cultural trends and practices. The battle between the sexes is an unfortunate result. Matthew Henry, the great Bible expositor, clearly understood how to put the husband-wife role problem into proper perspective. Writes Henry, "She was not made out of his head, to rule over him; nor out of his feet to be trampled on by him; but out of his side to be equal to him; under his arm, to be protected by him; and near his heart, to be loved by him."

> As unto the cord the bow is,
> So unto the man is woman,
> Though she bends him, she obeys him,
> Though she draws him, yet she follows,
> Useless each without the other!
> — Henry W. Longfellow

Notes

1. Roger J. Williams, *You Are Extraordinary*: Random House, 1967

2. Alfred Adler, *Understanding Human Nature*, p. 145

3. *Commentaries on the Laws of England*, p. 441

4. H. A. Ironside, *In the Heavenlies*: Loizeaux Brothers, p. 281

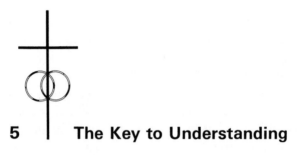

5 | The Key to Understanding

When Solomon began to write the Book of Proverbs, he might very well have had in mind young marrieds. For early in his great book he urges:

> Happy is the man that findeth wisdom, and the man that getteth understanding.
>
> For the merchandise of it is better than the merchandise of silver, and the gain thereof than fine gold.
>
> She is more precious than rubies: and all the things thou canst desire are not to be compared unto her.
>
> Length of days is in her right hand; and in her left hand riches and honor.
>
> Her ways are ways of pleasantness, and all her paths are peace.
>
> She is a tree of life to them that lay hold upon her; and happy is everyone that retaineth her.
>
> — Proverbs 3:13-18

You need no one to remind you of the importance of wisdom and understanding. It holds the key to successful human relationships. Surely no marriage can be successful without understanding. Most, if not all, marriage counselors agree that marital discord results in large measure from misunderstandings. The ability to communicate how we think and feel largely determines the reactions on the part of our spouses. Their reaction in turn is understood or misunderstood by us. When these actions and reactions are based on understanding, marital harmony results.

How is understanding promoted between husband and wife? By effective communication.

The most simple kind of communication is verbal. The first and possibly the most important thing to be noted here is this: Effective communication depends as much on the quality of *listening* as on the quality of speaking. You have probably heard the story that traces the communication development of a young couple. Before they were married, she listened while he talked. During the honeymoon, she talked and he listened. Afterwards they both talked and the neighbors listened.

Listening carefully and thoughtfully implies necessary qualities inherent in love relationships within the context of marriage. First, is implied *acceptance*. A desire to change behavior can only be produced if the person feels accepted *as he is.* How can one communicate acceptance to another who shows by what he does or does not do that he doesn't care enough to hear the person out? "He that answereth a matter before he heareth it, it is folly and shame unto him" (Proverbs

18:13). Rude interruptions and inattentiveness convey negative messages that strengthen resistance to change. The offended person usually feels that he must defend his position more than ever.

Closely allied to the quality of acceptance is *respect*. We communicate respect by being good listeners. The way that we listen shows in many ways how we feel about the one who is talking! Problems and differences, therefore, are resolved or magnified by the manner in which we learn to communicate acceptance and respect. And this is affected more by the way we listen than we might think. A ton of good psychology is contained in the advice of James: ". . . be swift to hear, slow to speak, slow to wrath" (James 1:19).

What are some useful suggestions on how we might promote understanding by the way we talk? Obviously what we say is important; so is what we don't say. Consider these indiscretions: "Of course, the only reasonable way to look at this is . . ." (implying that if you disagree, you are not reasonable). "Nobody can question this decision. . . ." (carrying the idea of rejection of anyone who might question the decision). "If you would only quit being so dogmatic about this. . . ." (suggesting that dogmatism is any position that differs from that of the speaker).

Regarding the importance of what not to say, it might be helpful to consider certain kinds of confessions. The marriage relationship can be weakened by the wrong kind of "skeleton exposures." Sometimes memories of acts committed before marriage produce strong feelings of guilt. Perhaps confessing to one's mate would make the confessor feel better, but what kind of burden would this impose on the other party? Is withholding a questionable or lurid affair from one's mate a lack of honesty and openness which should characterize the marriage relationship? Most authorities feel that it is better to let your relationship rest on what it has become since the beginning of your courtship with your mate. After all, it was from that point to the present that the basis of your relationship was developed. And further, to all who have genuinely repented of sin this promise can be claimed: "If we confess our sins, he is faithful and just to forgive our sins, and to cleanse us from all unrighteousness" (I John 1:9).

Not only is *what* we do and do not say important. *How* we speak deserves attention also. Emotions are easily recognized by voice tone. The author of Proverbs reminds us, "A soft answer turneth away wrath, but grievous words stir up anger" (Proverbs 15:1). Consider what must have happened when these words erupted in a husband-wife skirmish:

> My love, I'm sure the guy
> Was brilliant as you say —
> Far cleverer than I, no doubt,
> Because he got away.

Nonverbal communication is also a factor in a stable marriage relationship. A good illustration of what we mean comes from the experience of a young married couple. They agreed upon a system whereby each would know when the other needed special attention and understanding. The husband said, "When I come home with my hat on backwards, you'll know that I've had a rough day." The wife agreed and added, "And when you come home from work and see that my apron is on backwards, you'll know that I've reached the end of my rope."

Things worked very well for a while. When the husband came home with his hat on backwards, his wife was unusually thoughtful and helpful. At the end of the day, when the wife met her husband with her apron on backwards, she was treated with the utmost courtesy and consideration. For a while the system worked to perfection. Then one day the husband came home with his hat on backwards, and his wife met him at the door with her apron on backwards, too!

An additional point needs emphasizing. We are growing in the art of communication when we go beyond thinking about what we are or are not going to say. We must also consider the possible *effects* of our communication on our partner. "How will he see this?" "If I put it like this, will she understand?" "How can what I want to say be worded so that chances of being misunderstood and/or offensive will be reduced as much as possible?"

We communicate how we feel about each other in many subtle ways. Love or the lack of it can be communicated by a touch, a look, a gesture, an act as well as by words. Sensitive Christian marriage partners guard against communicating, either verbally or nonverbally, coarseness, inconsideration, callousness — all of which create barriers to growth in oneness. This verse by Edna St. Vincent Millay deserves memorization:

Tis not love's going hurts my days,
But that it went in little ways.

Marriage succeeds or fails in terms of trivialities; communications involve handling those trivialities. Therefore, if we neglect the art of communication, it will be to our increasing sorrow.

In this connection we remember the marriage failure of Thomas Carlyle, a satirical author and philosopher. Jane, his devoted wife made special efforts to show her love for her famous husband. Carlyle never communicated how he appreciated her delicious meals and other services. He allowed his work to consume so much of his time and attention that his wife was shut out of his life.

In spite of this neglect Jane continued to attend to her husband's needs and wants. Then one day at the table, she asked him why he never praised her for the efforts she made to please him.

"Woman," he rudely retorted, "must you be paid for everything you do?" Then he rose from the table and shut himself up in his study.

After Jane's death in 1866, Carlyle was sorrowfully going through her belongings when he discovered a diary. He sat down and slowly turned the pages. On many of the pages he noticed that the ink had been blurred by what must have been tears. A closer look revealed that often the stains were on statements that had a heart-breaking theme:

Oh, if only you would say something nice to me and show that you appreciate what I do for you! I am so hungry for a bit of praise from you.

It was raining when the gruff literary genius made his way to his wife's grave. He knelt on the rain-soaked clay and sobbed, "Oh, Jane, would that I had only known."

Perhaps he never had put himself in his wife's place. Perhaps he was so preoccupied with his own needs and interests, he failed to understand that because he did not communicate love and appreciation he had put his wife on an emotional starvation diet.

Whenever husband and wife interact, they communicate. Growing in this ability to express and react so that understanding is promoted will be a rudder that can guide your marriage safely through potentially destructive waters. "A word fitly spoken is like apples of gold in pictures of silver" (Proverbs 25:11).

Dr. William C. Menninger points out that discussions can be aided by "having a sense of humor; proper timing; not putting a partner on the defensive; not talking when too angry or upset; not letting the problem fester too long; and making a strong effort to understand what the other person is trying to say."[1]

In I Peter we read a warning to married couples. We must guard against that kind of interaction that breaks our communication with God. This we must do "that our prayers be not hindered" (6:7).

Dr. Samuel Shoemaker made it clear, however, that even in Christian homes there is imperfection. The place of effective communication that he gives in his description of the Christian home is impressive. Dr. Shoemaker writes:

> A Christian home is not one in which the relationships are perfect . . . but one in which the imperfections and

failures are acknowledged and where problems are worked out in prayer and obedience to the light God sends. In such homes there is great freedom for people to say what they think and express what they feel. There is not the repression of law imposed by one or both of the parents on the children, nor by somebody's temper or tears on everybody. People are allowed to grow up, to make mistakes to be themselves, to laugh, to live through difficult crises or periods with privacy if they want it, with help if they want that.[2]

Maturity has been defined as the ability to live in someone else's world. This requires being able to put oneself in the place of another, to feel as he feels, interpret as he interprets. The path that leads to this kind of understanding is not traveled in one day or one week. Neither can the traveler be spared certain pains and disappointments. But who would hesitate when one perceives the rewards of this "way of understanding?"

Notes

1. *Living In A Troubled World*, p. 21, 22
2. Samuel M. Shoemaker, *With the Holy Spirit and With Fire*: Harper and Row, p. 121

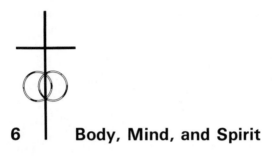

6 Body, Mind, and Spirit

How does marriage differ from other enduring human relationships? Basically the difference can be explained in terms of a full-dimensional expression of mutual commitment. By "full-dimensional" I mean all three aspects of the human personality — body, mind, and spirit. All this is contained in the Biblical word *knowledge*, which is used to describe the deepest, most intimate kind of husband-wife relationship. Prior to marriage, the Christian couple establish a partial-dimensional relationship, in that their becoming one has consisted of the merging of mental and spiritual aspects of personality. The marriage relationship is not consummated until their union includes complete sexual expression of their love.

A lack of understanding of the Biblical position regarding the physical expression of becoming one flesh probably accounts more than anything else for the many problems married couples report in this area. In a recent study, for example, married couples ranked sexual problems number one in terms of the length of time required for making a satisfactory adjustment.

If you look in the Bible for *sexual intercourse, coitus,* or other synonyms you will be unsuccessful in your search. This is true, not because this subject is too delicate — the Bible cannot be rightly accused of being evasive in matters of importance to man's search for the full life. Instead of speaking of marriage in terms of sex (which means the state of being male or female), the Bible speaks of it in terms of knowledge. "And now Adam knew his wife, Eve, and she conceived . . ." (Genesis 4:1). In this way maximum meaning is given to the sexual experience. When husband and wife become "one flesh" through the physical union, much more is involved than sexuality. Howard Whitman has written:

> The essence of love is intimacy. This means the closeness which makes two hearts beat as one, one mind almost supernaturally conscious of another mind, one set of emotions so tuned to and responsive to another set of emotions that feelings are intermingled if not fused.[1]

Scripture speaks of sexual intercourse in terms of knowledge because it is through the physical union that oneness in its *total sense* is experienced. The involvement is rational, emotional, and spiritual as well as physical. Coming together as man and wife has profound symbolic meaning. Rightly understood, sexual relationships are indeed sacred. Thus this form of "knowledge" is sacramental in nature, embracing and uniting body, mind and spirit.

All this should be clear, but it must be remembered that ours is a culture in which false notions abound. Growing up in such a society subjects one to various kinds of errors that subtlely enter the mind, affecting one's pattern of living. As a professor once stated, "It's not what we don't know that hurts us so much as what we are sure we know but don't."

Nowhere does evidence for this position display itself more conspicuously than in the area of sexual adjustment in the marriage relationship. Large amounts of time are spent by every marriage counselor dealing with victims of false ideas absorbed from others.

The New Testament provided a clear and pure source for the stream of thought in regard to the physical union between man and wife. Perhaps the most comprehensive word was given us by the great Apostle Paul:

> The husband should give his wife what is due to her as his wife, and the wife should be as fair to her husband. The wife has no longer full rights over her own person, but shares them with her husband. In the same way the husband shares his personal rights with his wife. Do not cheat each other of normal sexual intercourse, unless of course you both decide to abstain temporarily to make special opportunity for fasting and prayer. But afterward you should resume relations as before, or you will expose yourselves to the obvious temptation of the devil — I Cor. 7:3-5, Phillips.

These verses clearly indicate that both husband and wife have sexual needs. The coital experience has been referred to as "something the man enjoys and the woman endures," but there is no Scriptural basis for that attitude. As C. S. Lewis says:

> Christianity is almost the only one of the great religions which thoroughly approves of the body . . . if anyone says that sex, in itself, is bad, Christianity contradicts him at once.[2]

Negative attitudes have polluted the pure stream of Christian teaching regarding physical expression of love. Dean Inge, Anglican scholar and writer, traced the notion that the body and all its functions are impure, to Oriental influences. Among some other tributaries that fed poison into the stream was Gnosticism. Because of the half-truths taught by these pseudo-spiritual leaders, emphasis was placed on glorifying abstinence from and renunciation of physical pleasures. Dean Inge quotes an early historian who said, "It was expressly enjoined that no married persons should participate in any of the great church festivals if the night before they had lain together."[3] Actually it was not until the Reformation that organized religion began restoring true dignity to the marriage relationship.

Jesus declared, "Ye shall know the truth and the truth shall make you free" (John 8:32). Today more than ever, we need a clear word of truth in this area to free us from the confusion and our bondage to error. No clearer word is available to modern Christian couples than the simple, authoritative statement given by the writer of the Book of Hebrews: "Marriage is honorable in all, and the bed undefiled" (Hebrews 13:4a).

A Christian sociologist has recently written a book

that every engaged and married Christian couple should read. Its title is *Sexual Happiness in Marriage*. The author, Herbert J. Miles, believes that ignorance of the sexual aspect of marriage is inexcusable and that modesty is inappropriate in the coital experience. Questions of frequency of coitus, positions and love play are wisely answered in terms of what people find mutually pleasurable and satisfying. He explains that according to Divine intention, the physical union should nourish, strengthen and ennoble the marriage relationship.

Every married Christian should understand that the same love that *limited* the oneness of the relationship before marriage now *looses* each partner in joyful surrender to complete oneness.

> Let thy fountain be blessed: And rejoice with the wife of thy youth. Let her be as the loving hind and pleasant doe; let her breasts satisfy thee at all times; and be thou ravished always with her love (Proverbs 5:18, 19).

The vital role that the spiritual dimension plays in expression of married love (not love-making) has been recognized by contemporary psychiatrists and psychologists. From the famous Swiss psychiatrist, Paul Tournier, comes this insight:

> Without God, the regulation of the sex life in marriage is either a compromise in which each partner hides his real thoughts from the other, or else tyranny of one over the other, or it may be an artificial and rigid edifice of formal principles. No moral or psychological system can regulate by principles a domain which belongs to daily obedience to God, to the free submission to him of the

conscience enlightened by the Scriptures and the teaching of the Church. When God directs the sex life of a married couple, they can practice it divinely, if I may use the word — in a full mutual communion that is carnal, moral, and spiritual all at once. It is the crowning symbol of their total giving of themselves to each other.[4]

For those who link piety with prudery it should be pointed out that no one derives as much mature and exalted pleasure from the sex act as Christian couples. Christian commitment, understanding of the art and techniques of expressing love, and patience and time spiced with a sense of humor enable married disciples of Jesus Christ to maximize the experience of becoming one flesh.

This chapter would be incomplete without mentioning that one of the major functions of marriage is reproduction. Family planning is a subject of major importance to engaged and married couples. For a couple to mutually desire children is an indication of maturity and good marital adjustment. However, the questions of how soon after marriage should one become a parent, what means of controlling birth should be used, and how child-spacing should be determined need to be thoroughly discussed and understood. Responsible parenthood may be defined in terms of the child's welfare. Will he be adequately loved, protected, cared for, educated? Am I as the parent ready to become responsible for providing a model for my child to imitate? Is my marriage stable enough to enable an addition to the family to have *his* needs adequately satisfied?

BODY, MIND, AND SPIRIT   53

The major burden of this chapter, however, is that of emphasizing that the physical aspect of becoming one is a function of total personalities. When the Christ-centered personalities of husband and wife merge through sexual contact Divine as well as human blessing results.

Notes

1. *The American Way of Love,* p. 10
2. C. S. Lewis, *Mere Christianity;* Macmillan, p. 77
3. W. R. Inge, *Christian Ethics and Modern Problems*
4. Paul Tournier, *The Healing of Persons*: Harper and Row, p. 179

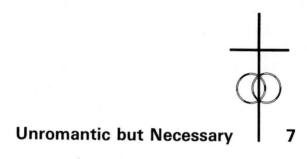

Unromantic but Necessary | 7

Christianity has been called the world's most material-
istic religion. This can be good news to the young
Christian couple who went into marriage thinking "two
can live as cheaply as one," and discovered they had
to add "but only half as long" to that statement.
"Give us this day our daily bread" is a request that
many young marrieds learn to take quite seriously.

There might have been a time when financial solv-
ency and other related problems would not have found
a place in a book of this type. But research into the
causes of marital unhappiness is focusing a great deal
of attention on economics. Landis, for example, found
that adjustment in money matters required a larger
period of time than any other kind of problem except
sex relations.[1]

Marriage as partnership is a principle that should be carried out in the area of paycheck spending and saving. Probably every couple should work out a plan that best serves their unique needs. Learning to be wise stewards of your income may require a great deal of wisdom, patience, effort — and not a little prayer! As one man noted, "Enough is always a little more than what you have." We all join with O. W. Holmes, who wrote:

> I care not much for gold or land —
>   Give me a mortgage here and there —
> Some good bank stock, some not of hand,
>   Or trifling railroad share —
> I only ask that fortune send
>   A *little* more than I shall spend.

Actually, for Christians, material wealth, at least to the degree that our needs are supplied, is a serendipity. Christ was not unaware of man's needs in the material realm. His words in this matter are not those of a mere visionary whose concern was so heavenly he forgot about things earthly:

> No man can serve two masters; for either he will hate the one, and love the other; or else he will hold to the one, and despise the other. Ye cannot serve God and mammon.
>
> Therefore I say unto you, Take no thought for your life, what ye shall eat, or what ye shall drink; nor yet for your body, what ye shall put on. Is not the life more than meat, and the body than raiment?
>
> Behold the fowls of the air: for they sow not, neither do they reap, nor gather into barns; yet your heavenly Father feedeth them. Are ye not much better than they?

Which of you by taking thought can add one cubit unto his stature?

And why take ye thought for raiment? Consider the lilies of the field, how they grow; they toil not, neither do they spin:

And yet I say unto you, That even Solomon in all his glory was not arrayed like one of these.

Wherefore, if God so clothe the grass of the field, which today is, and tomorrow is cast into the oven, shall he not much more clothe you, O ye of little faith?

Therefore take no thought, saying, What shall we eat? or, What shall we drink? or, Wherewithal shall we be clothed?

(For after all these things do the Gentiles seek:) for your heavenly Father knoweth that ye have need of all these things.

But seek ye first the kingdom of God, and his righteousness; and all these things shall be added unto you — Matthew 6:24-33.

Those who make pleasing Christ their central aim in life have His promise that what they truly need they shall have. This does not mean, of course, that human responsibility can be cast away. Indeed, if one possesses the Spirit of Christ, his policy will be thrift and hard work, which is the Protestant Ethic.

Care should be taken lest thrift be taken too far. Sometimes wives complain, "Just because I don't work outside the home my husband thinks I shouldn't have regular amounts of money to spend." Husbands and wives will be interested to find out what researchers at New York's Chase Manhattan Bank have estimated the worth of a wife to be. They calculate that the average housewife works a 99.6-hour week. This is broken down as follows: 44.5 hours as a nursemaid

($1.25 an hour), 5.9 hours as a laundress ($1.90), 13.1 hours as a cook ($2.50). This puts the housewife's weekly pay at $159.34 — and this is not counting overtime for work beyond 40 hours. This means that, at competitive rates, most housewives would earn as much as their husbands.

To discuss in detail such matters as how and when to buy homes, cars, clothes, insurance, etc. would not be within the scope of this book. However, these general points may prove helpful:

1. Remember that patterns of spending and value systems are developed over a long period of time and do not change easily and quickly.

2. Budget your income. Be realistic about limits for spending. Talk with your partner about what your necessities are and are not. Plan together.

3. Develop an effective filing system. Over a lifetime hundreds of dollars can be saved by wise, accurate and consistent filing of receipts, canceled checks, deductible items, and important business papers. Both partners should be familiar with the system. My wife and I have found that the two dollars we spent for a box file was one of our wisest investments. It is divided into monthly sections and includes space for deductible items and other spaces for checks, bills, etc.

4. Let the control of the purse strings be determined by demonstration of good judgment rather than how it reflects on the role of either partner.

5. Plan for the future. The three financial periods of life have been identified as (1) learning years (up to

age 25), (2) the earning years (from 25 to 65), and (3) either the yearning or the golden years, depending on the way you managed during the earning years. According to statistics, out of 100 people reaching age 65, two are financially independent, 23 continue to work, 75 depend on friends, relatives, or charity for their livelihood.

Perhaps John Wesley's sermon on Christian economics will summarize the main points. He exhorted his listeners to make all the money they could, save all the money they could, and give all the money they could to help extend the Kingdom of God.

Financial responsibility is directly related to emotional and spiritual maturity. The use of money is also a reflection of one's philosophy of life. The meaning given money quickly exposes whether one's values are properly placed.

In his book *Fifty Years With the Golden Rule*, J. C. Penny credits his wife for being instrumental in helping him achieve national recognition for his chain of department stores:

> From the moment I married, I had a real helpmeet. Many a night when she sensed that I wanted to keep on working at the store she packed my supper in a tin pail and brought it to me. Very often she supplied me with hints about how to add service and value from the woman's point of view, and I felt that, whatever position of independence I might grow to in the future, in my wife I had my first and invaluable partner.

Nowhere in all literature is the importance of the wife's character, competence and industry to the suc-

A Virtuous Woman

Who can find a virtuous woman? for her price is far above rubies.

The heart of her husband doth safely trust in her, so that he shall have no need of spoil.

She will do him good and not evil all the days of her life.

She seeketh wool, and flax, and worketh willingly with her hands.

She is like the merchants' ships; she bringeth her food from afar.

She riseth also while it is yet night, and giveth meat to her household, and a portion to her maidens.

She considereth a field, and buyeth it: with the fruit of her hands she planteth a vineyard.

She girdeth her loins with strength, and strengtheneth her arms.

She perceiveth that her merchandise is good: her candle goeth not out by night.

She layeth her hands to the spindle, and her hands hold the distaff.

She stretcheth out her hand to the poor; yea, she reacheth forth her hands to the needy.

She is not afraid of the snow for her household: for all her household are clothed with scarlet.

She maketh herself coverings of tapestry; her clothing is silk and purple.

Her husband is known in the gates, when he sitteth among the elders of the land.

She maketh fine linen, and selleth it; and delivereth girdles unto the merchant.

Strength and honour are her clothing; and she shall rejoice in time to come.

She openeth her mouth with wisdom; and in her tongue is the law of kindness.

She looketh well to the ways of her household, and eateth not the bread of idleness.

Her children arise up, and call her blessed; her husband also, and he praiseth her.

Many daughters have done virtuously, but thou excellest them all.

Favour is deceitful, and beauty is vain: but a woman that feareth the Lord, she shall be praised.

Give her of the fruit of her hands; and let her own works praise her in the gates.

— Proverbs 31:10-31.

cess of marriage so eloquently praised as in the last chapter of Proverbs.

Concern for finances is normal, but we must not lose our balance. Our interest in material gain can be so absorbing that we lose out on life's finer blessings. A fascinating illustration of what can happen when man tries to live by bread alone appeared in the sports section of the Houston Post.[2] Harve Boughton, the author, told of meeting an old friend named "Trombone" Sledge at the annual sports show. "Trombone" was one of a colorful group of retired old salts whose fishing interests and other circumstances brought them together. The group came to be known as the "Barge Boys," because they lived in a barge-shack in the Marsh near the intracoastal canal.

At first the Barge Boys made their living by catching fish with rod and reel and marketing their catch. They were old pros at catching fish and soon were making a handsome living.

Then they got the idea of raising trout, redfish, flounder and even shrimp in the marsh lake. Within six months, their salt fish hatchery had netted them eighty thousand dollars.

When the writer paid his next visit to the Barge Boys' hangout, he was not prepared for what he saw. They were not a little tipsy and were engaged in destroying their fish hatchery. When asked what was going on, Trombone explained, "See how beat up we are! You never saw such a fight as we stupes got into yesterday. It was coming for a long time. We'd been arguing over nothin' at all, but mostly about that . . .

hatchers and the big money we was makin'. When we got through with that brawl yesterday, we sat around lookin' at each other kind of stupid-like, wonderin' what was happenin' to us and remembering how it used to be around here, when we was just going out fishing and havin' fun and likin' each other."

The sportswriter was then led to the scene of destruction. Trombone pointed to the 24-foot turbo-jet barely visible in the water. Five holes had been blown in the hull of the boat by a shotgun. Now there was no fish hatchery and no sleek turbo-jet. The Barge Boys had learned that "life consisteth not in the abundance of things that a man possesseth." Instead of letting the money-craze destroy their relationship, the poorer but wiser and happier trio decided to chart a new course. As one of them said, "We goin' back to livin.'"

Being able to postpone satisfaction of needs in order to achieve a more worthy goal in the future is a mark of maturity. At those times when some self-denial is necessary it helps to remember these can be opportunities for growth. And besides, temporarily "doing without" can be far from dull as the poet points out:

> They're planning to get married, and I'm rather glad they are.
> Although the road ahead today seems difficult and far.
> They've very little money, and I'm rather pleased at that;
> They'll know the joy of striving in an inexpensive flat.
>
> They're launching out together with high hopes and courage great.
> They'd dreamed of having riches, but they've chosen not to wait.

And they're starting out with little — just his salary every
week,
And they'll have to save and struggle now for every
joy they seek.

Their bills will give them trouble, and they'll sigh for
things in vain;
She's going to do the cooking, and I fancy 'twill be plain.
He'll help her in the kitchen, and he'll dry the dishes too,
And learn a lot of duties which he never thought he'd do.

But every chair they purchase will be laden with delight;
Every trinket toiled and saved for will with joy be doubly
bright.
So I'm not the least bit sorry, but am positively glad
For they'll know the fun of striving which their Dad
and Mother had.[3]

Notes

1. Judson T. Landis and Mary G. Landis, *Building a Successful Marriage,* 5th ed., © 1968: Prentice-Hall, Inc., Englewood
Cliffs, N.J., p. 361
2. *Houston Post,* Sunday, July 21, 1968
3. Theodore F. Adams, *Making Your Marriage Succeed*: Harper and Row, pp. 88-89

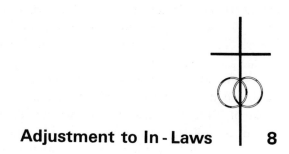

Adjustment to In-Laws | 8

In my courtship and marriage class a number of students appear startled when I say to the class, "You don't just marry your mate; you marry his family, too!" The significance of this aspect of marital adjustment is indicated by some research by Judson and Mary Landis. They questioned 544 young married couples and found that in-law relationships headed the list of difficult areas. Some of the complaints were:

> They try to run our home.
> They treat us like children.
> They give us too much advice.
> They try to help us too much.
> They hover over us.

In the Landis study, the mother-in-law received most of the blame, with the husband's mother drawing more complaints than the wife's mother. Incidentally, the Seminole Indians of Florida have a unique way of temporarily handling the mother-in-law problem. They have found that tea made from the dieffenbachia plant can have a peculiar effect on the person who drinks it. It seems that the nerves in the tongue are deadened. When mother-in-law drinks the potent brew her scolding tongue is silenced for four or five hours! Thus the Seminoles have named the dieffenbachia the "mother-in-law plant."

In general, indictments against mothers-in-law certainly do not hold true. Robert E. Lee, for example, spoke of his mother-in-law, Mary Curtis, like this: "She was to me all that a mother could be, and I yield to none in admiration for her character, love of her virtues, and veneration of her memory."

One form this in-law problem can take was discussed in the *Houston Post*. An upset young husband wrote to Billy Graham whose knowledge of the Bible enables him to give authoritative answers. Here is the question and Dr. Graham's answer:

> QUESTION: My wife is very jealous of my mother, and I always side with my mother when they have an argument. My wife thinks I love my mother more than her. Am I wrong in doing this? W.H.J.
>
> ANSWER: Yes, you are wrong in taking your mother's side in an argument, instead of your wife's. The Bible says, "Therefore shall a man leave his father and mother, and shall cleave unto his wife: and they shall be one flesh" (Gen. 2:24).
>
> I have the most wonderful mother-in-law in the world, and she, wisely, doesn't defend her children if they are wrong. You say that you "always side in with your

mother." No matter how good your mother is, she couldn't possibly be right all the time. Even if she were, you should stand by your wife, for the Bible says you are to "leave your mother, and cleave to your wife." A sure way to marital suicide is to always take the side of your parents against your wife.

Most mothers-in-law are wonderful people, and the way to be a wonderful mother-in-law is to not be overcome with emotion, but to look at disagreements fairly and objectively. It is natural to defend one's flesh and blood, but as mature adults, we are to be motivated by what is right, not what one wants to be right, even if it's wrong.

Stand by your wife, even if it offends your mother. You are only asking for trouble if you do otherwise. Of course, there may be times when your wife is wrong, but this should be discussed in private, when your mother is absent.

Every mother and father need to remember what being a daughter-in-law or a son-in-law is like. And daughters- and sons-in-law can profit by studying some Biblical examples.

Take Ruth, for example. Her relationship with her mother-in-law, Naomi, should serve as a model for modern mother- and daughter-in-law relationships.

Ten years after Naomi had suffered the loss of her husband, she lost her two married sons. This great loss left Naomi alone in a strange land. She decided to return to Judah, the land of her countrymen. Volumes of thought on in-law relationships are contained in the Biblical episode that took place at Naomi's leaving:

And Naomi said unto her two daughters-in-law, Go, return each to her mother's house: the Lord deal kindly with you, as ye have dealt with the dead, and with me.

And they lifted up their voice, and wept again: and Orpah kissed her mother-in-law; but Ruth clave unto her. And she said, Behold thy sister-in-law is gone back unto her people, and unto her gods: return then after thy sister-in-law. And Ruth said, Intreat me not to leave thee, or to return from following after thee; for whither thou goest, I will go, and whither thou lodgest, I will lodge: thy people shall be my people, and thy God my God: Where thou diest, will I die, and there will I be buried: the Lord do so to me, and more also, if aught but death part thee and me."

— Ruth 1:8-17

The remainder of the Book of Ruth is a living testimonial to the blessings that can accrue to an in-law relationship because of a common faith in God. This is the formula for building a family structure that will endure.

Difficulty with parents and in-laws can sometimes be explained by examining the psychology of adolescent development. Adolescence is the concentrated seven-year reach for independence. To the teen-ager growing up means becoming one's own boss. Hopefully one's perspective keeps broadening because marriage is very difficult for those who continue to cling to the ideas of independence which include freedom from emotional ties. Those who seem to adjust most effectively think not in terms of independence but of interdependence. An understanding of the concept of interdependence enables the married couple to avoid being overly dependent on their parents and at the same time to avoid the other extreme, that of thinking "we're on our own now, so leave us alone."

Landis quotes two statements from young married

persons that serve as excellent illustrations of healthy and maturing attitudes toward parents. A young husband writes:

> My mother welcomed us with open arms after our honeymoon and was just full of ideas on how to help us. She would load us down with food of every imaginable sort, slip me five dollars for fuel for our car, which she also gave us. The payoff came when, after I mentioned, merely conversationally (I thought), that our mattress had a broken spring, she wrote and said she was bringing us a new one. Margaret hit the ceiling and said Mother would never let us be independent if this kept up. She was certainly right, yet I could not help but realize that I, myself had, unconsciously spurred my mother on. I knew that I depended entirely too much on my mother, and I realized that I had to change in order to have a satisfactory marriage. My mother was the victim, for as I would never have done before, I called her and told her as nicely as I knew how that we could not possibly accept the mattress. She protested, saying that she enjoyed doing what little she could to help us. But help was not the issue; my maturity was the issue. If I accepted the mattress, there would be similar things I would be accepting. For some time my mother was deeply hurt, and I was deeply hurt over the whole situation.
>
> But eventually my mother came to realize that perhaps she had interfered somewhat, even though she had tried to help us. I now look back and view the situation as constructive, a trivial situation to an observer perhaps, but a major step toward our independence and my maturity.

And this from a young wife:

> I have had an adjustment to make — that of psychologically leaving my family's home. Before I was mar-

ried, I was very close to my family, especially my mother. When I got married, however, I found that if things did go wrong for a day or so, I owed it to myself and to Jerry not to go home with the problem. If Jerry and I had an argument and I took my side of it to my mother and father, they would be inclined to take my side, and would find it hard to forgive Jerry easily, as I could do after we had solved the problem and made up. As time goes on I have come to understand that I no longer need to depend so much on the love and security that my parents gave me, for I have my husband and our home. (But it's still nice to know my parents are there.)[1]

Parents often wonder how they can help newlyweds without hindering. And the newlyweds search for ways to "cleave" together without making their parents feel completely rejected.

Do you recall the Old Testament account that involved Moses and his father-in-law, Jethro? A lesser man than Moses might have been offended when, during a visit with his famous son-in-law, Jethro said to him, "The thing that thou doest is not good" (Exodus 8:1). Jethro's statement referred to what Moses had been doing in a superhuman effort to help his people with their many problems. From daylight to dark Moses was devoting all his time to being the counselor to an entire nation.

Observing his son-in-law's impossible task, wise old Jethro counseled Moses with these words: "Hearken now unto my voice, I will give thee counsel, and God shall be with thee." Jethro suggested that Moses delegate authority to wise, godly men who would assume responsibility for judging the people. Only the problems of greatest importance would be brought to Moses.

Moses could have rejected this counsel from his father-in-law. Fortunately, Moses had no need for proving that he was responsible and able to manage his affairs by refusing to consider the possibility that perhaps he could use some advice. Moses' reaction proved him to be a wise man, for the Bible states, "So Moses hearkened to the voice of his father-in-law, and did all that he had said (8:24). The happy result was that Moses' leadership became more extensive and effective than before.

Nothing reveals a person's wisdom more quickly than how he reacts to correction. The Bible reminds us of this with statements like these:

Faithful are the wounds of a friend.
— Proverbs 27:6

Rebuke a wise man and he will love you.
— Proverbs 9:8

These are not to be taken as directives to become humanity's throw-rug. When circumstances and situations call for it, firmness is in order. Some have found it necessary to deal firmly with in-law problems that threatened their marriage. Moreover, newlyweds are obeying God when they shift their deepest loyalty from parents to each other. However, even when outside interference threatens, you will do well to remember, "if it be possible, as much as lieth in you, live peaceably with all men" (Romans 12:18).

The fact is that both sets of parents *and* their married children have certain kinds of adjustments to make.

From your point of view, you must consider whether or not the in-laws are Christans. It is a vital factor in the causation of problems and how they are confronted. Was your marriage approved by both sets of parents? If not, additional time will be needed to develop more harmonious relationships. Sincere effort made in this area pays big dividends. You must also determine the degree of acceptance or non-acceptance by in-laws.

In-laws must ask themselves the following questions: Does our married son or daughter still need us? Will our desire to help them be misinterpreted? If problems between us arise will they feel free to come to us and "clear the air?"

At least two big *don'ts* should be noted: (1) *Don't* argue in the presence of your in-laws. Sides will be taken. Indiscreet comparisons are often made and this creates resentment which erects barriers. (2) *Don't* criticize your mate's parents, even if your mate is doing it. This is usually done in heated moments. When calm times arrive, evaluations are made of what was said and from stored-up memories. Future interaction with those same in-laws will be affected by what has been said in the past. Exercising discretion on these two points is an investment in the future of your marriage.

The way we live over a period of time identifies us as wall-builders or bridge-builders. When the Spirit of Christ operates in our relationships, we become bridge-builders. Besides, those who build walls have special problems. They must realize what they are walling in, as well as what they are walling out.

Modern marriages would be almost entirely free of vexing in-law problems if everyone involved would manifest the kind of love that Paul describes in the famous love chapter:

> Love is very patient and very kind.
> Love knows no jealousy;
> Love makes no parade, gives itself no airs, is never rude, never selfish, never irritated, never resentful;
> Love is never glad when others go wrong,
> Love is gladdened by goodness, always slow to expose, always eager to believe the best, always hopeful, always patient.
> Love never disappears.
>
> — I Corinthians 13:4-8, Moffatt

If we have this kind of love we are ready to join with Paul when he says a few verses farther in the chapter:

> When I was a child, I talked like a child, I thought like a child, I argued like a child; now that I am a man, I am done with childish ways. — 13:11, Moffatt

Notes

1. Judson T. Landis and Mary G. Landis, *Building a Successful Marriage*, 5th ed., © 1968: Prentice-Hall, Inc., Englewood Cliffs, N.J., p. 335

9 | **Your Marriage as Ministry**

A man was strolling beside a construction job and noticed three men hard at work with their shovels. "What are you doing?" he asked the first man. "I'm digging a ditch," the man growled. The same question was asked of the second man who replied, "I'm earning my salary." When the third man was asked what he was doing, he replied with gusto, "Mr., I'm helping to build a cathedral!" All three men were doing the same thing, but how different was their conception of the importance of what they were doing!

How blessed is that marriage in which each partner possesses an exalted conception of the purpose of life in general and of marriage in particular! Married life does not have to degenerate into boredom, divisions, or meaninglessness. On the contrary, when both husband and wife look upon their marriage as a means through which the living Christ can witness to this lost planet, their union takes on its highest purpose. Then marriage will not be a malady, but a ministry!

How our world needs the ministry (service) of dedicated husband and wife teams! Signs of decay are evident and have been for some time. Two generations ago, Oswald Spengler in his *Decline of the West* aimed this stinging indictment at America and Europe:

> You are dying. I see in you all the characteristic stigma. I can prove to you that your great wealth and your great poverty, your capitalism and your socialism, your wars and your revolutions, your atheism and your pessimism and your cynicism, your immorality, your broken-down marriages . . . that is bleeding you from the bottom and killing you off at the top in the brains — I can prove to you that these were characteristic marks of the dying ages of ancient states — Alexandria and Greece and neurotic Rome.[1]

One symptom of decay in our society is the fact that mental health has been called our number one problem. For example, little did Mary Hayworth, author of a syndicated newspaper column, expect what would happen when she replied to a man who had asked where he could get psychiatric help. In her answer she suggested that he write to Dr. George S. Stevenson, Medical Director of the National Committee for Mental Hygiene. After the reply the NCMH was swamped with more than two thousand letters, coming from forty-five states and from Puerto Rico, New Foundland, and Nova Scotia. The problems mentioned in the letters ranged from neurosis and psychosis to pregnancy out of wedlock, marital difficulty, educational and vocational problems.[2]

In the light of all this, how filled with impact are the words from the great Apostle Paul to Timothy, his spiritual son:

> This know also, that in the last days perilous times shall come. For men shall be lovers of their own selves, covetous, boasters, proud, blasphemous, disobedient to parents, unthankful, unholy, without natural affection, trucebreakers, false accusers, traitors, heady, high-minded, lovers of pleasure more than lovers of God; having a form of godliness, but denying the power thereof: from such turn away — II Timothy 3:1-5.

Could it be that your marriage has taken place in the generation that will witness the second appearing of Christ? Could it be that your marriage like that of Esther of generations long ago was brought into existence "for such a time as this?" (Esther 4:14)

The late President John F. Kennedy warned, "Today, every inhabitant of this planet must contemplate the day when this planet may no longer be habitable. Every man, woman and child lives under a nuclear Sword of Damocles, hanging by the slenderest of threads, capable of being cut at any moment by accident, or miscalculation or by madness." Granted, this is an hour of crisis. But let us be reminded that when written in Chinese, the word crises is composed of two characters — one represents danger; the other opportunity. Christian couples like you and your partner have an unprecedented opportunity to contribute to a society that is desperately in need of the ministry of your marriage.

The same Elizabeth Barrett Browning who penned the hauntingly beautiful lines about her love (see chapter 1, p. 7) also wrote:

> Earth's crammed with heaven
> And every common bush afire with God;
> And only he who sees takes off his shoes, —
> The rest sit round it and pluck blackberries.

Dr. Lynn Harold Hugh said, "The trouble with our world is this: People are giving first class loyalties to second class causes."

The need of the hour may have been expressed in these throbbing words:

> O God, when our time seems short
> and our responsibilities seem long
> and our mood is heavy, full of pressure,
> grant us a great thought.
>
> O God, when we count the days before us
> and the days behind,
> but when their effort seems for trifles or for naught,
> when our habits and our patterns and relationships
> bind our lives with cutting but invisible chains,
> grant us a great thought.
>
> Grant us again, O God, a great thought
> when sorrow drops upon us,
> when situations make us worriers instead of warriors,
> when we are weary with programs
> and with projects and with people.
>
> And Father, in the circumstances where we stand alone,
> judged by ourselves but not enough forgiven,
> shaken by the loneliness of never being fully compre-
>   hended

or even cared about or listened to,
grant us then, O God, another great
sustaining thought.

O God, whose works are open but whose workings
hidden
when we look into the context of our world
and our experience,
when we see our possibilities
and our impossibilities
and are ready, not to rest and rise again,
but to resign,
save us from the silent shriek of our surrender,
uplift us with that hand that out of darkness
flung out light,
and for the sake of those whose lives are structured
in the art or artlessness of ours,
do thou, O God of all our expectations and endurance,
grant us a great thought.[3]

Shortly after graduation from Southern Bible College, Fred and Jo Carol Duncan became missionaries to Indonesia. Upon their arrival this capable, dedicated husband-wife team immediately involved themselves in the Bible college program that trains the native Christians to become effective Christian witnesses to their own people. Their letters told of their work and how happy they were knowing that God's will for their lives was being realized.

Time passed and then word was received regarding a Communist take-over attempt in Indonesia. Little did Fred and Jo Carol Duncan realize that the Communists had drawn up a list of names of persons to be "eliminated" when the conquest was over. The names of the Duncans were reportedly fourth and fifth on that list.

Rev. Don Shute, responsible for foreign missionary programs, quickly made the trip to Indonesia and took each of the Duncans aside for private discussions. He explained to Fred and Jo Carol that their lives were in danger and that if they wanted to return to the States it would certainly be understandable. When Rev. Shute returned to America, he told with tear-filled eyes and unsteady voice how they individually replied. Fred was sure that he wanted to stay where God had called him. Jo Carol unhesitantly replied, "This is where my husband and I have our work. I won't say that I'm not afraid but the Lord who called us here is able to take care of us. If it pleases Him to allow otherwise, then so be it. We want the will of God to be done." They stayed and miraculously escaped the would-be captors who were themselves captured before they could carry out their horrendous plan.

I bring this little book to its close by inviting you to consider with me this matter of understanding marriage as ministry. Without sparing ourselves let us ask ourselves, "What is my purpose for living? How will my life as a married person be evaluated by Him who loves me and gave Himself for me? Am I fully surrendered, totally commited to — dare I say it — reproducing the life of Jesus Christ on earth?"

The degree to which we can answer these questions, especially the last one, is the degree to which we will grow in conformity to Christ. As we grow in conformity to Him, we also grow together in truly becoming one flesh as married partners. Growing in Him produces increasing oneness regarding the marriage relationship.

And by its very nature this process of becoming one is, in its most noble and dignified sense, an adventure.

> "Life is so very different!"
> they said, (now they were man and wife.)
> "Wonder what's out there ahead of us?"
> they asked, (now they were looking at life.)
> And then they saw an open road,
> And Someone wondered, "Will they?"

Notes

1. Oswald Spengler, *Decline of the West*: Alfred A. Knopf, Inc., 1926

2. S. W. Gansburg, Troubled People, *Mental Hygiene*, 32:4-14

3. Lona Fowler, *Concern*, February, 1964